TENNIS FASHION

© 2003 Assouline Publishing
601 West 26th Street, 18th Floor
New York, NY 10001 USA
Tel.: 212 989-6810 Fax: 212 647-0005
www.assouline.com

Translated and adapted from the French by Ilona Bossanyi

ISBN : 2 84323 438 7

Color separation: Gravor (Switzerland)
Printing by Grafiche Milani (Italy)

TENNIS FASHION

DIANE ÉLISABETH POIRIER

ASSOULINE

The Edwardian age of tennis

When Major Walter Clopton Wingfield patented the new game he called *"sphairistike"* in 1874, he had no idea that his invention would meet with such phenomenal success. Astutely, he had revived and codified the rules of lawn tennis, which had become popular among the English aristocracy a few years before. The new sport was the exclusive preserve of an affluent, leisured elite, and was played in the most select clubs of the land. Lawn tennis was a modern adaptation of the well known "jeu de paume", a game played at the Royal Court of France since the Renaissance.

LEFT: a woman tennis player around 1905, in a romantic long-sleeved blouse and long striped skirt—but her chignon is daringly uncovered.
ABOVE: Major Walter Clopton Wingfield.

In a stroke of genius, Major Wingfield designed a box to hold a kit that included the rules of the game along with all the necessary equipment: stakes, net, rackets, balls and line markers. He established the size of a tennis court at 18.40 metres long and 9.40 metres wide, with a net 1.42 metres high. In just a few years, his "portable" tennis game had conquered the world and was played in the most far-flung British colonies.

It was not long before the game became a competitive sport, with official rules established as follows by the All England Croquet and Lawn Tennis Club in 1877:

— A tennis court had to be a rectangle measuring 23.77 metres by 8.23 metres.

— Points were counted as fifteen, thirty, forty, game, advantage and deuce.

— The height of the net was set at 0.92m.

Within a few months, championships were being organised at Oxford and Cambridge universities, and the first Wimbledon tournament took place that same year.

Lawn tennis caught on equally fast along the East Coast of the United States, thanks to Miss Mary Outerbridge who brought the first tennis kit from England in 1874. After the first official American championships in Newport in 1881, the young champion, Dwight Filley Davis, launched a three-day men's tennis tournament that was played in teams between different countries. The game gained popularity across the Atlantic with the first

ABOVE: Australia's Tennis City in 1923. The White City tennis club in Sydney consisted of 46 tennis courts. Australian players soon showed exceptionally good form in international tournaments, winning the Davis Cup as early as 1907. OPPOSITE: case for tennis outfits designed by Louis Vuitton.

Davis Cup, won by the USA in 1900. Tennis had come into fashion. Its increasing popularity created entirely new sectors of activity. For example, the first India-rubber tennis balls were too soft, and were replaced for the first Wimbledon tournament by rubber balls covered in four segments of white wool sewn together (today, more than 30,000 balls are used in each Wimbledon tournament).

Players were free to choose the size of their rackets and mesh and the length of the handle. By 1900, Slazenger already had a wide range of models in its catalogue.

The craze for lawn tennis spread throughout Victorian high society, and was boosted still further by the later invention of the lawn mower. Before long, owners of country houses were rushing to turn part of their grounds into tennis courts. Lawn tennis was fast overtaking its rival in elegant leisure pursuits: the inevitable game of croquet after a summer picnic. No garden party was complete without the classic call of "tennis, anyone?"

Gentlemen in jackets, cuff links, cravats and flannel trousers began to adopt the striped monogrammed blazer that marked them out as members of the same tennis club during a match.

Gallantly striding out onto the courts came tightly corseted Edwardian ladies in wide-brimmed, beribboned hats, petticoats and ankle-length skirts aswirl, stockings and laced booties staunchly forbidding the merest glimpse of a bared ankle. The one concession their costume might make to sport was an apron with a wide pocket to hold their tennis balls.

NEXT PAGES: typical Edwardian tennis players about town, the men in long-sleeved shirts, dark trousers and straw boaters, the ladies in long skirts, tightly corseted waists, leg-of-mutton sleeves, white booties and cloche hats.

Although pale colours were recommended as more suitable in the heat of summer, white was by no means the rule: the fashion for tennis whites was launched by Maud Watson, the winner of the 1884 Wimbledon ladies' tournament.

In France, lawn tennis first appeared in Le Havre, then in Dinard, and went on to conquer the whole of the Atlantic coast. The first French championships took place in Paris, in 1891.

As the twentieth century dawned, tennis was all the rage in the smart sports clubs of the café society, but was also being played in a more casual manner in Atlantic seaside resorts and on the grounds of the charming villas of the Riviera. "The Riviera in the morning is for all the world like a giant tennis court, with cries of 'Ball!' in Hyères, echoed by calls of 'Play!' in Menton", according to the April 1902 issue of *L'Illustration*.

Baron Pierre de Coubertin actively contributed to the growing craze for tennis, by founding the Etretat Tournament and especially by having tennis included as an Olympic discipline at the 1900 Olympic Games in Paris, where the first French women's tennis champion, Hélène Prévost, took on the British champion, Charlotte Cooper, in a spirited match.

Sarah Bernhardt would play tennis each day during her vacations on Belle-Ile. Marcel Proust took great interest in the tennis parties organised by Parisian clubs. Tennis became all the rage among young Parisian women, although their games were hardly professional— during the finals of the French championships at Puteaux, the winning contestant actually gave up the game to be sure not to miss a society dinner engagement!

The fashion pictures in *Femina*, *La Vie au grand air* or *L'Illustration* helped the spread of tennis fashion by gradually persuading women to wear more fluid garments.

Femina

Mlle BROQUEDIS
Championne de Tennis aux
Jeux Olympiques.

PIERRE LAFITTE & Cⁱᵉ, 90, Champs-Élysées, Paris.

Cover of the 15th August 1912 issue of Femina magazine, showing Mademoiselle Broquedis, the Olympic women's tennis champion, in full swing. The style is fairly casual: round-necked, collar-less blouse with elbow-length sleeves, skirt hem just above the ankles, little hat with coloured taffeta ribbons, white stockings and pretty shoes laced with a big bow.

11

By 1904, full tennis outfits were on offer in stores like Tunmer or La Belle Jardinière in Paris.

Tennis players gained more freedom of movement as they abandoned tailored armholes and constricting flannel jackets.

The first men's champion who imposed his personal style in tennis clothing was Max Decugis, in 1902. A health-conscious man who hated to catch colds (antibiotics had not yet been invented), Decugis would don a heavy raglan-sleeved overcoat and a huge scarf at the end of each match. His sporting figure and brilliantined hair added to his reputation as a charmer. His style, as the top-seeded French tennis player, quickly caught on both on the courts and in town.

Wealthy tennis players would order their tennis kits from Louis Vuitton and have their racket covers made to order by Hermès. Their thinly striped flannel trousers made their way into gentlemen's fashion as "tennis flannels".

Ladies took to bulky, knitted sleeveless pullovers with ribbed welts in contrasting colours, the forerunners of the classic tennis sweater with its striped V-neck. Rubber-soled canvas "sneakers" took over from booties.

LEFT: Mildred Davis in 1926, displaying the sophistication of 1920s tennis fashion in carefully applied make-up and a round-collared sweater.

RIGHT: the modest tennis ball has changed over the century in texture but very little in size. The yellow TV-friendly tennis ball is currently the official favourite.

NEXT DOUBLE-PAGE: lawn tennis case with rackets, stakes, net and balls, as designed by Major Wingfield when he took out the patent in 1874. (Roland-Garros Tenniseum collection.)

COURS DE LAWN TEN

The Roaring Twenties

Tennis came bounding back into fashion immediately after the First World War. The euphoria of new-found peace sent the affluent classes into a whirl of leisure pursuits: flying tennis balls consigned four nightmare years to oblivion. With luxurious liners crossing the Atlantic in under a week, international tennis tournaments were soon organised. In 1920, sensing the potential of tennis, industrialists began to take a keen interest in players' needs. New brand names like Superga (1923) and Spring Court (1936) launched into the promising new market with improved rubber-soled tennis shoes, while Babolat, Tunmer, Dunlop and Slazenger designed new high-performance balls and rackets.

July 1925, the French tenniswoman Suzanne Lenglen in the Wimbledon finals for the sixth time. In outfits by Patou, her inimitably graceful acrobatics would mesmerise her opponents.

Audience of all times: during Roland-Garros in 1929 (right): spectators actually remove their jackets in the heat of the moment; in the Wimbledon stadium in 1932 (above), bowler hats and little pillboxes.

NEXT PAGES: LEFT: a pretty tennis tunic with rackets embroidered on the front, specially created by Hermès in 1927.
RIGHT: by the 1920s, the most famous Paris fashion houses were designing tennis fashions, like this pretty boat-neck dress created by Jeanne Lanvin in 1922.

A timeline of tennis rackets: here is its evolution from 1900 to nowadays, from the irregular strings and the curved handles to the advanced technology and the synthetic fibres.

Наприне

As women's emancipation and the tomboy style gathered strength, ladies' tennis boomed, with Suzanne Lenglen as the new tennis heroine.

With her dazzling victories, "the Divine Lenglen", as she came to be known, marked the turning point between the tennis of the Twenties and the game we know today.

With scant regard for her reputation, Lenglen had the couturier Jean Patou create a revolutionary tennis outfit: in a pleated knee-length skirt and sleeveless cardigan. Her hair held by a wide tulle head-band, she embodied the ideal of a whole generation and became a symbol of women's emancipation.

She was the first true star of tennis, a celebrity whose fame spread well beyond the sports chronicles. Photographed by her friend J.H Lartigue and trained by her father who would dope her up on the courts with swigs of brandy, she regularly played against the cream of the men's tennis aristocracy, like Gustave V of Sweden or the famous navigator Alain Gerbault. When she retired from competitive tennis, she took the helm of the Yvonne May fashion house in 1930, but sadly died of leukemia at the age of 39.

Like Patou, who established a sportswear department in 1922, Jacques Heim, Jeanne Lanvin, Jane Regny, Rochas, Schiaparelli and Hermès were soon creating gorgeous little silk dresses and accessories to meet the growing taste for tennis among their clientele.

Taking over from the pleated skirt, divided skirts appeared in 1932. The world of Haute Couture invaded the courts, and the tennis style became all the rage, with plenty of room for the most wildly extravagant tastes. The Spanish women's champion Lili d'Alvarez won her victories at the Wimbledon and Roland-Garros tournaments in a jewel-encrusted red and gold dress, while Chanel jersey suits strolled around club lawns and city streets.

PREVIOUS DOUBLE-PAGE: a 1936 illustration showing the main tennis strokes.
NEXT PAGES: LEFT : Monte-Carlo: King Gustave V of Sweden, a keen amateur player, embodies the aristocratic elegance of tennis. RIGHT: the stunning Spanish player Lili d'Alvarez in full swing at Wimbledon in 1927, daringly sporting a divided skirt with little flounces.

Coco Chanel herself would stride around the courts to admire the men in her life, until 1938 when her fiancé Paul Iribe collapsed and died of a heart attack.

Change was also on the march in women's tennis fashion on the other side of the Channel. Alice Marble revolutionised tenniswear at Wimbledon in 1933, playing matches in shorts and shirts like those worn by female students in America. The style created a modern silhouette that was completely new to Europe and quickened the pulse of a generation.

Women tennis players took to socks instead of stockings, rolling them down over their tennis shoes to show off tanned limbs. Clothes became simpler and more comfortable.

Lacoste, Borotra, Cochet and Brugnon, the four Davis Cup winners from 1927 to 1932, best exemplify men's tennis fashion in the Roaring Twenties.

Cravats and jackets gave way to ample white shirts, sometimes worn with the sleeves rolled up. Borotra's Basque beret and espadrilles became his trademark on the courts, and Lacoste set his own trend with his famous cap. After matches, the "four musketeers" would shrug into big white V-necked sweaters with stripes at the collar and cuffs. Confirming the new relaxed fashion, tennis players from Monaco to Long Island adopted an artfully casual style that came straight out of F. Scott Fitzgerald's novels.

This was the golden age of French tennis.

The international Roland-Garros stadium, built in Paris in 1928 to host the Davis Cup finals, was splendidly inaugurated by the victories of all four musketeers.

In 1933, Lacoste put aside his tennis racket to launch his own business, designing the first of his polo shirts with the famous Lacoste crocodile logo, and a tennis ball throwing machine.

PAGES 28-29: LEFT: a tennis outfit from around 1935: short-sleeved shirt and shorts decorously fastened with buttons at the waist. RIGHT: a tennis dress from the 2002 collection designed by Le Coq Sportif with the Belgian player Justine Hénin (under exclusive contract). This stretch model in Coolmax (polyester with Spandex) is bacteria-resistant and breathable for optimum comfort during the exertions of a championship match.

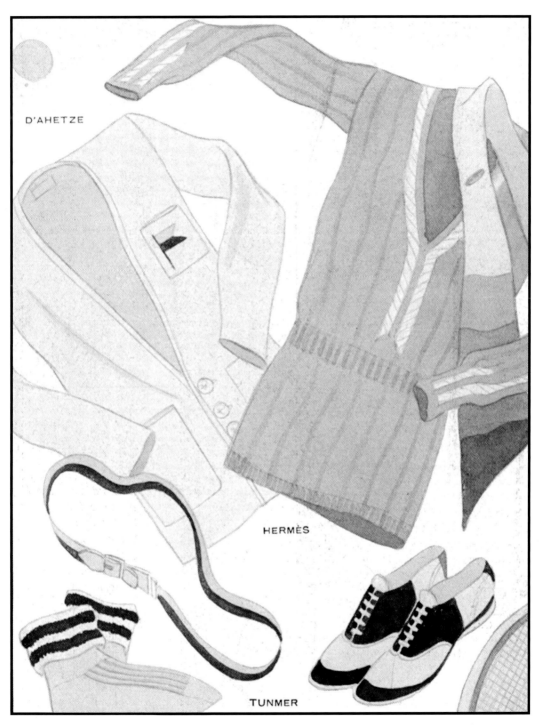

D'AHETZE

HERMÈS

TUNMER

LEFT: Henri Cochet at Wimbledon in 1923; Suzanne Lenglen at Wimbledon in 1920, in one of her famous short dresses by Jean Patou; the Frenchman André Merlin was the first tennis player to wear the famous Lacoste polo shirt; the American Donald Budge during a 1937 Davis Cup match.
RIGHT: from the *Jardin des Modes* fashion magazine (June 1930). Tennis fashion had become a must in women's spring wardrobes.

The same year, the British player Fred Perry took the Wimbledon Cup and became a symbol of British tennis chic.

Perry and Austin, who also wore shorts on the courts, won the Davis Cup back from the musketeers and revived the fortunes of British tennis. Like Lacoste, Fred Perry also founded his own clothing company.

In the USA, the irresistible charm of the Californian tennis player Donald Budge drew full-capacity crowds, with fans emulating his style. These new icons of an entire generation became the ambassadors of newly international fashions in sportswear. The Grand Slam and Davis Cup tournaments brought dreams of glory to champions and amateur players alike, and set the pace of their sophisticated life-styles.

At the end of the Thirties, the emerging clothing industry began to take an interest in the sportswear market. Tenniswear departments appeared in the major European and American clothing stores. But the boom came to a sudden halt with the outbreak of the Second World War.

The return of the champions

American tennis was hit less severely by battles and rationing, and like Australian tennis, blossomed quickly in the aftermath of the war. The team spirit of tennis clubs in American universities and their intensive coaching programmes helped to forge a generation of champions.

Nevertheless, class barriers remained, and the gap widened between amateur and professional tennis. Playing tennis still meant paying club membership dues and owning expensive equipment.

PREVIOUS PAGES: LEFT: 1927, René Lacoste loses to Takeichi Harada at Forest Hills in the U.S.A. His friend Robert George drew the crocodile which he later had embroidered on his blazer. RIGHT: 1933, René Lacoste creates the Lacoste polo shirt, named "1212", with André Gillier, a draper from Troyes. OPPOSITE: Bunny Austin launched the fashion for shorts during the 1933 international tournament at Forest Hills.

Most clubs still banned Black people and foreign religious denominations from their courts.

Amateurs with enough time and money to play tennis were not paid when they played tournaments, though they did receive gifts from sportswear manufacturers. The age of sponsorship had begun.

As the battle raged between amateurs and professionals, the international tennis scene of the 1950s was mainly dominated by Australians, although famous Australian players like Frank Sedgman, Lew Hoad, Ken Rosewall and Rod Laver were banned from the major championships when they turned professional. Despite fervent pleas in favour of professional tennis from the American players Bobby Riggs and Jack Kramer, the issue was not resolved until 1965.

Off-the-rack tennis fashion

In the 1950s, amateur and professional players set a trend for more casual tennis fashion, with shorts and short-sleeved polo jerseys. The classic tennis shirt gradually disappeared as René Lacoste's short-sleeved polo shirts in 100% cotton jersey swept the board.

Their success encouraged many manufacturers to experiment with varying amounts of synthetic fibre in their short-sleeved polo shirts. These included the string vest from Rasurel, Fred Perry's polo shirts and the short-sleeved tennis shirt from Le Coq Sportif.

By 1946, shorts had won the day, and in the 1950s, men's tenniswear took to the streets, with items like the polo shirt becoming a fashion basic in every man's wardrobe.

Tenniswear changed with advances in synthetic fibres. Materials became softer, lighter, easier to care for and more comfortable to wear. Styles were increasingly varied.

The celebrity of tennis champions began to attract off-the-rack clothing manufacturers.

In 1965, Le Coq Sportif launched a tenniswear line and became the official sponsor of the French champion Patrick Proisy.

In 1966, the Italian champion Sergio Tacchini retired from a splendid career to create his own label. As pure white tennis clothes continued to reign supreme on the courts, his coloured outfits were a total innovation. His daring designs hit the fashion scene like a bomb and became the first success for his brand.

The same year, Horst Dassler's company Adidas designed the first tennis shoes in leather, named the "Robert Haillet", together with Le Coq Sportif. In 1966, the brand became the French Tennis Federation's first sponsor, staunchly supporting the likes of Georges Goven and Florence de la Gontrie.

The tennis courts became a battleground for companies like Fila, Adidas and Spring Court, as they competed for the booming market in tennis shoes.

NEXT DOUBLE-PAGE: Gussy Moran, nicknamed "Gorgeous Gussy", was an outstanding champion as well as the woman behind the couturier Teddy Tinling. The sight of her lace-frilled knickers caused a scandal at Wimbledon in 1949. Pictured here playing a match at Madison Square Garden, Gussy Moran caused another sensation at the same venue with panties in leopard-skin print.

Frills and glamour

1950s tennis also boosted the women's clothing
market. A generation of increasingly emancipated
and athletic young women particularly enjoyed the
freedom afforded by short hemlines. Their taste
for sport brought these young baby-boomers to
demand other products. In her short, flared skirt
and sleeveless shirt in white cotton piqué, Maureen
Connolly, nicknamed "Little Mo", embodied all
the charm of American youth. Sportswear designers
adapted the tennis style to the dictates of fashion,
with padded shoulders in 1948, the Princess line
in 1952, baggy shorts in 1958, big round buttons
in 1960, giant zips in 1965, mini-skirts in 1966...

OPPOSITE: winner of the Wimbledon, Rome and Forest Hills championships, the beautiful Brazilian
Maria Bueno turns fashion model for Teddy Tinling, the most famous tenniswear designer, in 1966.
NEXT PAGES: LEFT: 1953, film poster for *Mr. Hulot's Holiday*. RIGHT: Gussy Moran strolls along Piccadilly
before her first Wimbledon match in 1949.
PAGES 44-45: LEFT: 1965 tennis lingerie. RIGHT: close-up of Mlle Billat de la Courbie's short skirt
during the Porée Cup match in September 1963.

rené péron

Women shook off tennis traditions much faster than men. Althea Gibson was the first Black winner of a major title, in the 1956 French championships, but Arthur Ashe only won the U.S. Open in 1968, after years of heroic battle to gain acceptance. His ultimate success finally opened up tennis to everyone.

From 1959 to 1966, South American tennis came into its own, as the Brazilian player Maria Bueno won titles in all the major events. The impeccable, sophisticated style of her short pleated outfits brought a taste of high glamour to tennis fashion.

Advertising for cosmetics, sun-tan products, accessories and cigarettes made good use of the attractive image of women tennis players. Tennis was definitely the "in" thing in the sixties.

The women's tennis circuit became increasingly well-organised, thanks to Billie Jean King, the American women's champion. Her tenacious efforts were rewarded by the creation of the WTA, Women's Tennis Association, supported by Virginia Slims.

In France, fashion received a boost from Françoise Dürr, the first French winner of the Roland-Garros women's championships. As a mixed sport, tennis found particular favour with a generation of young people who still went to single-sex schools but would turn up in gangs at the tennis clubs, zooming up on their Vespas with the wind in their hair.

In Paris, as the events of May 1968 simmered in the wings, Courrèges, Pierre Cardin, Balmain and Pierre d'Alby each brought out a range of high-fashion tennis outfits, with torso-hugging polo shirts for the men and very short skirts that completely bared shapely feminine thighs.

Adidas began a spectacular ascent with the "Stan Smith" tennis shoe, named after the famous champion. As 1972's number-one seed and fast court specialist, Stan Smith and his impressive performances helped the company sell thousands of pairs.

The age of Open tennis

In 1968, amateur and professional players finally buried the hatchet, and the age of Open tennis began. A great many players and organisers had helped to bring this about, giving a tremendous boost to tennis worldwide. In 1968, in France, thanks to the efforts of Philippe Chatrier, the French Internationals at Roland-Garros became the first Grand Slam tournament in which amateurs and professionals played the same matches.

The tremendous growth of Open tennis that began at that point was largely due to Björn Borg.

His achievements (49 consecutive victories in 1979 alone) are unequalled to this day, and Borg is still one of the brightest stars in the tennis firmament.

With their flair for the winning streak, the Italian sportswear companies were the first to attach their brand image to an international champion. Fila launched a sponsorship scheme with Borg in 1973. Following their lead, the American company Head named their first fibreglass tennis racket after Arthur Ashe. McEnroe signed a partnership contract with Sergio Tacchini in 1978, and Vilas followed suit with Ellesse in 1980.

Sales were no longer driven by the name of a champion, but by the image of a champion's brand.

People bought Fila sportswear to identify with Björn Borg, but also because they saw the technology invested in the item as contributing to his success. (On retiring from competitive tennis, Borg launched his own sportswear brand, but had to liquidate after only a few months). Marketing had entered the world of Open tennis.

The fascination of Borg's supreme mastery of the courts found its equal in the elegance of the British champion Chris Evert.

NEXT PAGES: LEFT: the American Stan Smith, an ace player on the clay courts, on the Wimbledon grass court during the 1971 tournament. As the number-one seed in 1972, he gave his name to the Adidas tennis shoe the same year. RIGHT: 22 June 1970, Arthur Ashe on the first day of the Wimbledon tournament. He wore an elegant turtleneck sweater and inaugurated a new kind of racket, made to his specifications by Head and called the "Arthur Ashe".

With her style and charm, Chris Evert became the embodiment of women's tennis in the 1970s. With the five million franc contract she signed in 1981 to wear the Italian firm Ellesse's navy blue pleated skirts on every tennis court on the planet, she became the forerunner of the fashion model tennis players of the year 2000.

In 1975, with a completely different style, the fabulous Martina Navratilova took over as the queen of world tennis. With 55 Grand Slam victories behind her (from 1975 to 1993), she felt no hesitation in walking onto the Wimbledon centre court in a simple pair of shorts. In 1983, however, obeying the dictates of English good taste, the Wimbledon Committee sent her off the courts because of her garish top! In the 1970s, cotton T-shirts and sweat-shirts from the USA swept into Europe, taking over the wardrobes and lifestyles of every sports-man and woman.

New textiles changed women's lives in particular, as "second-skin" underwear, unwired bras, jersey knickers and polyamide lace panties secretly helped them to victory.

Skin-tight shorts and polo shirts followed the latest fashions, while fans went wild over their champions' accessories: caps, eyeshades, headbands, wristbands in striped towelling—tennis shoes, the most popular item of all, which soon left the tennis courts to stride down city streets.

The war of the heavyweights

In 1980, all of chic Paris society crowded into the new temple of sport: the newly enlarged and renovated courts of Roland-Garros. With the most prestigious names in fashion inaugurating the tent village, sponsorship became official.

PREVIOUS DOUBLE-PAGE: Björn Borg, one of the greatest tennis champions of all time (49 successive victories in 1979) has inspired thousands of amateurs to try their hand at tennis. OPPOSITE: Chris Evert concentrates before taking on Virginia Wade at the 1977 Wimbledon finals.

ABOVE: view of the Roland-Garros central court, built within eight months for the 1928 Davis Cup.
BELOW: Flinders Park where the Australian Open has been played since 1993 on a hard surface known as Rebound Ace.

BELOW: view of the Arthur Ashe stadium at Flushing Meadow, the venue for the last of the four Grand Slam tournaments.
OPPOSITE: the centre court of the Monte-Carlo Country Club which was reputed as one of the most enjoyable tournaments and was also one of the oldest.

From 1981, the big names in tennis fashion began to hold court each year in Monte-Carlo. After Elie Jacobson created Dorotennis in 1978, a whole generation of designers launched into successful sportswear ranges: Daniel Hechter, Cerruti, Ted Lapidus, Gucci, Valentino, Dior and many more besides.

Logos vied for supremacy on every polo shirt, displayed by the Lacoste tribe, the Fred Perry team or the Ralph Lauren fan club. Men's fashions from Façonnable, Daniel Crémieux or Jeff Sayre hit the big time.

Tennis championships became media events, generating spectacular budgets. Spectators in the 1980s swooned over stars who played fast and hit hard.

After Björn Borg, the nerveless king of world tennis for over a decade, after watching Vilas and Orantes exchanging interminable volleys from the baseline, spectators delighted in Ilie Nastase's clowning, Pecci's ear-ring, Leconte's jokes and Connors' fits of anger.

The most charismatic champions were those who were capable of giving vent to their emotions on the courts. McEnroe's uncontrolled fits of temper hit the mark every time. Yannick Noah's tears of joy made him the hero of the day.

Noah's Roland-Garros victory in 1983 gave a tremendous boost to French tennis. His showmanship and the world of personal experience he brought to the courts made him the darling of every spectator. Captaining the French Davis Cup team in 1991, he got the entire stadium thrilling in unison to the reggae beat of *Saga Africa*.

When young André Agassi came bounding onto the courts, the spectators immediately fell for his grunge look. Shorts in bleached denim, bottom-hugging pants, long hair and flower-printed shirts — they loved it all.

OPPOSITE: 3 July 1974, the Romanian player Ilie Nastase clowning around during a Wimbledon match. NEXT PAGES: LEFT: the American Jimmy Connors in pretend agony after being hit by a ball from his opponent Vijay Amritraj during a match at Wimbledon in 1981. RIGHT: John McEnroe, the most rebellious player on the world tennis circuit, gives way to a fit of temper.

Agassi, like Noah and McEnroe, was one of that indomitable breed of players whose rebellious image became the key to the identities of brand names like Nike, Adidas, Puma and Reebok.

Tennis gear became the thing to wear: anywhere, at any time, in town or country. In turn, street gear leapt onto the courts with lead players like Agassi. Things were changing on the women's courts as well, as Monica Seles set her own trend with hoarse cries at every shot. Women's matches in the 1990s were played to the rhythmic panting and gasps of the girls' exertions.

Meanwhile, the battle of the brand names raged more fiercely than ever: stupendous contracts were signed with champions of both sexes. The big firms began to move away from traditional off-the-rack tennis outfits, establishing full-scale research laboratories to improve the performance of the products. With the advent of air-cushioned tennis shoes and "smart", breathable, antiperspirant fabrics, tennis fashions moved into the age of technology.

After the enfants terribles of the 1980s came a generation of champions, like Lendl, Becker or Sampras, whose performance hinged on technical perfection and efficiency rather than spectacular effects.

In the hands of managers like MacCormack, manufacturing tennis stars became a business. Players were subordinated to their brand names, flippancy and extravagance were banished to the sidelines. The success of Steffi Graf's solid, conscientious technique proved the point, but public enthusiasm waned.

Oddly enough, it was the new school that emerged from Eastern Europe after the fall of the Berlin Wall, with players like Kournikova and Safin, that signalled the revival of championship tennis.

OPPOSITE: Yannick Noah at the 1983 Roland-Garros Open: Falling to his knees on the clay court, the most expressive of all the French players created a show that sent the centre court at Roland-Garros—no French player had won the championships since 1946.
NEXT PAGES: LEFT: André Agassi, the other enfant terrible of American tennis. The "Las Vegas Kid" became famous in 1990 for his Grand Slam victories, but also for his streetwise look: long flowing hair, body-hugging fluo lycra pants, frayed bleached denim shorts and flower-printed shirts, all carefully put together by Nike. RIGHT: Gustavo Kuerten during Roland-Garros 2002.

The year 2000: tennis comes back to life

With materials technology now fully operational in the textile industry, style in tennis made a comeback through the strong personalities of a new generation of players. Jennifer Capriati's short, colourful skirts and Mary Pierce's rainbow tennis dresses had already hit the mark in 1998. With the new lycra-stretch fibre from Dupont de Nemours, women tennis players reached the star status of top models. Smashing their way to victory in their Nikes, Martina Hingis and Amélie Mauresmo generated sales far more effectively than any advertising campaign. The financial stakes were huge, and sponsors kept a keen eye on their champions' form and style.

Roland Garros in 1997: Mary Pierce was a magnificent example of the muscular image of world-class women's tennis.
NEXT PAGES: LEFT: Melbourne, 1995, Mary Pierce renewed the popularity of skin-tight tennis dresses with her scoop-necked sundress. RIGHT: Martina Hingis at Wimbledon in 2001, wearing the "one arm top" design developed by Adidas.

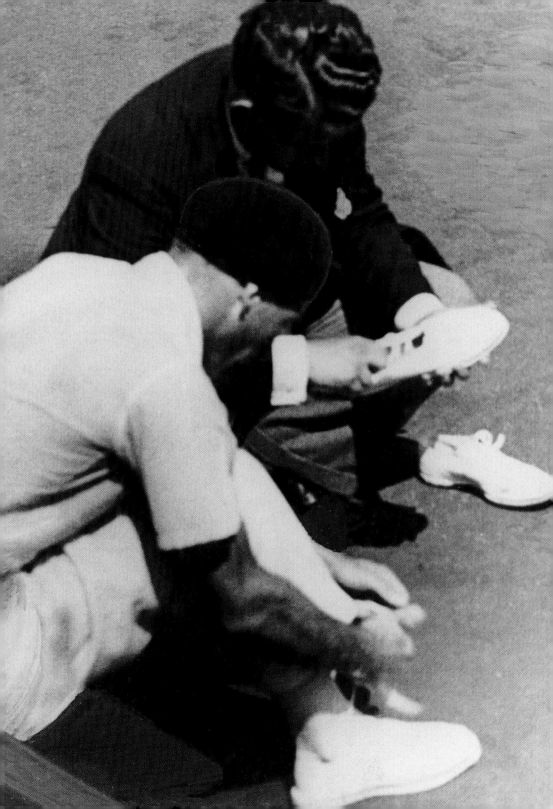

As the battle continued to rage between the major brands, prestigious designers of luxury off-the-rack fashions, like Chanel, Prada, Vuitton, Gucci or Dior, took a renewed interest in designing their own sportswear lines.

Thanks to the designer Christophe Lemaire, the famous "crocodile" logo became high fashion once again, from Paris to New York and from London to Sydney. Arnaud Clément added to the prestige of the brand with his succession of victories. With a bandanna tying back his flowing hair, wrap-around sunglasses and Lacoste polo shirts in every colour of the rainbow, Clément brought style back to French tennis. Adidas commissioned collections from the talented Japanese designer Yohji Yamamoto.

Streetwear bounded back onto the courts with lead players like Agassi, Kürten, Safin and Costa.

Today, each player expresses an individual style, with black socks and trainers, T-shirts and vests, overlong or baggy shorts.

Some look to the spectacular, like Serena Williams or the Brazilian champion Kürten, who wears football strips on the tennis courts.

Although tennis whites seem to have vanished into oblivion, the International Tennis Federation still keeps an eye on decorum: at Flushing Meadows, its officials sent Tommy Haas and his sleeveless T-shirt back to the changing rooms. Noblesse oblige!

PREVIOUS PAGES: LEFT: Jean Borotra, nicknamed the "bounding Basque", played all his matches in a Basque beret and espadrilles, as pictured here at Roland-Garros during the 1932 Davis Cup. RIGHT: Serena Williams' golden Puma trainer, during a match at the 2002 Roland-Garros championships.
OPPOSITE: the Williams sisters turned every match into a fashion parade, to the tune of the stupendous contracts they signed with their sponsors—Puma for Serena and Reebok for Venus in 2002.

Chronology

1874: Major Clopton Wingfield takes out a patent on the game of Lawn Tennis. He codifies the rules of the game and the size of the court, and designs a portable wooden case to hold nets, stakes, rackets and balls.

1876: First American Lawn tennis tournament organised at Nahant in the State of Massachusetts.

1877: First lawn tennis championships at Wimbledon.

1881: First American championships at Newport.

1884: The British tenniswoman Maud Watson wins the Wimbledon tournament to become the first women's tennis champion, and launches a new style in a pure white tennis outfit.

1891: First French Inter-club Lawn Tennis championships at Puteaux in Paris.

1895: Creation of the Paris Tennis Club.

1896: Tennis is recognised as an Olympic discipline (until 1924).

1900: Creation of the men's Davis Cup.

1901: First national tennis championships in Australia.

1913: The International Lawn Tennis Federation (now the I.T.F.) is founded in Paris.

1920: Suzanne Lenglen, wearing a tennis dress by Patou, wins the Olympic tennis championships in Antwerp, in singles and mixed doubles with Max Decugis.

1922: Jean Patou, Suzanne Lenglen's favourite dress designer, opens a sportswear department in his Paris fashion house.

1926: René Lacoste becomes the number one world seed.
Jeanne Lanvin launches a sportswear range in Cannes, Biarritz and Paris.

1927: The Roland-Garros stadium is built in Paris.

1927-1932: The "Four Musketeers" (Lacoste, Borotra, Cochet and Brugnon) win the Davis Cup six years running.

1933: René Lacoste creates the Lacoste polo shirt, with the reference number 1212.
The British tennis player Bunny Austin wears shorts at a tournament for the first time. The young American champion Alice Marble creates a stir when she plays for the Wimbledon Cup in shorts and a short-sleeved shirt.

1933-1936: The UK takes the Davis Cup four times in succession thanks to Fred Perry and Bunny Austin.

1938: The American Donald Budge becomes the first winner of the Grand Slam.

1949: Teddy Tinling becomes the tennis circuit's official designer, launching a line of sexy lingerie for Gussy Moran.

1956: Althea Gibson is the first ever Black player to win the French International Championships.

1959: Du Pont de Nemours patents Lycra as a brand name for its Spandex fibre. When woven with other materials, Spandex makes tennis clothes more supple and comfortable.

1965: Le Coq Sportif launches a tenniswear line and becomes the official sponsor for the French champion Patrick Proisy.

FROM TOP TO BOTTOM AND FROM LEFT TO RIGHT: the Roland Garros cup; the famous silver-gilt Wimbledon cup; the Davis Cup; the Monaco Cup.

1965: Le Coq Sportif links up with Horst Dassler's German brand, Adidas.

1966: Adidas creates the first leather tennis shoe, called the "Robert Haillet". On retiring from an outstanding international career, the Italian tennis player Sergio Tacchini creates his own sportswear brand, revolutionising the sector with coloured tennis outfits.

1967: Tennis whites go into terminal decline. The French player Françoise Dürr wins the French championships at Roland-Garros and launches the fashion for tennis mini-dresses.

1968: Tennis goes Open with the French international championships at Roland-Garros, where amateurs and professionals play together for the first time.
Arthur Ashe wins the US Open.

1969: Adidas launches a tenniswear collection designed for Ilie Nastase, Harold Solomon and Eddie Dibbs. Tennis shirts with the Adidas triple stripe first appear on the courts.

1972: The American player Stan Smith gives his name to the new tennis shoe from Adidas.

1974: Björn Borg wins his first major victory at Roland-Garros in a white outfit with fine navy stripes and Fila's famous red and blue F logo.

1978: The US Internationals move from Forest Hills to Flushing Meadow.
Elie Jacobson designs his first sportswear collection and launches the Dorotennis brand.

1981: Daniel Hechter creates Daniel Hechter Sport and opens boutiques specialising in his own designer label.
Chris Evert signs a spectacular, exclusive five million franc contract with Ellesse to wear the brand's tennis clothes on every court on the planet.

1983: The French player Yannick Noah wins his first triumphant Grand Slam victory at the finals of the French international championships at Roland Garros.

1988: Fila, Adidas, Ellesse and others launch their new tenniswear lines for women, in stretch lycra.

1989: Reebok presents the "Impulse" lightweight tennis shoes for clay courts, worn by Michael Chang and Arantxa Sanchez in their winning matches at Roland-Garros in 1989.

1990: Asics creates its first textile collection, although champions had been wearing brand-name tennis shoes since 1960.

1992: Agassi launches the grunge look in tennis, wearing Nike colours.

1994: Reebok perfects its tennis shoe range with the "Insta Pump" triple inflatable membrane, providing incomparable lightweight support.

1995: Reebok becomes the exclusive supplier of tennis outfits to the young champion Venus Williams.

2001: Asics becomes the official tennis shoe supplier for the Davis Cup.

2002: Tommy Haas is sent off at the Flushing Meadow championship in New York, for wearing a sleeveless T-shirt.
Reebok develops the new DMX Lite technology, with a system of hollow cells giving a maximum cushioning effect along the whole foot. Worn by Venus Williams during championship matches, the shoe seems to have vindicated its designer's claims.

With her Slavic charm, Anna Kournikova: clad in short shorts and stretch bra, her sexy glamour did wonders for Adidas (in 2002) way beyond the tennis courts

Bibliography

Amson, D., *Borotra*, Tallandier, 1999

Borg, Björn, *Revers*, Michel Lafont, 1993

Chevalier, J.P., *Le Tennis à l'affiche*, Albin Michel, 1986

Clerici, G., *500 ans de tennis*, Hatier, 1976

Clerici, G., *Lenglen, la diva du tennis*, Rochevignes, 1984

Dunkley C., *Le Tennis*, Flammarion, 1998

Garnier, G., *Paris Couture, années 30*, musée Galliera, 1987

Lacoste, René, *Plaisir du tennis*, Fayard, 1981

Leconte, Henri, *Ma vie de gaucher*, Solar, 1993

Noah, Yannick, *Secrets, etc.*, Plon, 1997

Talliano F., *La Villa Primrose, un siècle d'histoire sportive*, Confluences, 1997

Tauziat N., *Les Dessous du tennis féminin*, Plon, 2000

Valleriaux F., *Le Tennis et l'Objet*, L'Albaron, 1990

Eurosport, *Guide*, Promedi, 2000

Other sources : *Adam* and *Femina* magazines,
*Elle, l'Équipe, La vie au grand air, L'Illustration,
Jardin des Modes, Tennis magazine, Vogue.*

Special thanks to Isabelle Aimone, Claire Venambre and Jean-Christophe Piffaut
of the Roland-Garros Tenniseum for supporting the author in her research
and for allowing her to use the French Tennis Federation's archives.
The author is also most grateful to the Couture establishments
and the press officers of the fashion and sportswear designers
who made their archives and documentation available to her, especially:
Adidas (Marie Gérard and Laurence Firmian), Asics (Sonia Weber-Zmirov),
Chanel (Cécile Goddet), Le Coq Sportif (Virginie Meyer, Christel Proust),
Daniel Hechter (Carine Falke), Dorotennis (Catherine Vinson),
Fila (Cyril, Catherine North), Hermès (Nathalie Vidal), Lacoste (Catherine Pietri),
Lanvin (Odile Fraigneau), Nike (Stéphane Sigaud), Reebok (Patricia Menant),
Rossignol (Christophe, Brigitte Chouet),
Sergio Tacchini (Patricia-Laurence Phitoussi),
Louis Vuitton (Marie–Sophie Carron de la Carrière).

The publisher wish to thank Ciné-Images,
Thierry Freiberg (Corbis), Isabelle Sadys (Keystone),
Audrey Snell (Wimbledon Law Tennis Museum).